MY FAITH WALK

FROM BLESSING TO BLESSING

ZULEKHA I. JONES

"Attention: Permissions Coordinator"
Infinity Publications, LLC.
Vanderbilt Media House, LLC.
999 Waterside Drive
Suite 110
Norfolk, VA 23510
(804) 286-6567

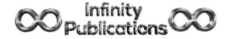

ISBN-13 : 978-1-953096-20-3
Library of Congress Control Number: 2021923620
Paperback First Edition: February 2022
10 9 8 7 6 5 4 3 2 1
Scriptures marked KJV are taken from the KING JAMES VERSION (KJV):
KING JAMES VERSION, public domain.
www.vanderbiltmediahouse.net
Book printed in the United States

My Faith Walk

Table of Contents

My Acknowledgments

I would like to give the highest honor to my Heavenly Father- God and to his son Jesus and to the Holy Spirit for bringing me through every season of my life up to this present time. I know without all three of them would not have made it through these challenging times in my life.

A Special thanks go out to my mom, Mabeline. I would like to say thank you for all you have done and still doing for me. Thank you for always being there for me even when you were exhausted with life duties. Mom, you still take time out to make sure I am alright. I'm truly grateful for your unconditional love, support, and advice. Thank you for taking care of me when I was unable to take of myself when I was a child and even when I fell gravely ill a few years ago. Mom, you are a Phenomenal Woman! Love your daughter, Zulekha.

Special thanks to my Dad Ellis for teaching me how to tie my shoe when I was seven years old. Thank you for your continued love and financial support. I am forever grateful. Love, your daughter Zulekha.

Specials thanks go out to my brothers, Knowledge and Rod. You both mean a lot to me. Knowledge thank you for encouraging me to continue to write this book especially during the times when I was unmotivated to write. I am forever thankful for the countless words of wisdom you shared with me. I love you always, your big sis Z. Rod, thank you for never failing to share a funny story with me from our past managing to make me laugh whenever I was down. I also thank you Rod for always being around to pick me up when my legs were too tired and for being my personal bodyguard and so much more. I Love You always, Z.

Many thank you goes out to all my Aunties, Uncles, family, and friends who have been there for me throughout my life. I am blessed to have you all in my life.

To my Beloved mom-mom Nellie. You will always hold a special place in my heart. I remember you would always share my birth story and how tiny I was with everyone you came in contact with. Now that you are no longer here on earth mom-mom Nellie, I have to continue to tell the rest of my story. Love you always. Your granddaughter, Zulekha.

To my beloved grandfathers, Roger Polk, Sr., and Ellis Taylor. You both will forever hold a special place in my heart. I will always remember the good times we shared together and the lessons you two have taught me as well as the stories you both have shared with me. I love and miss you always. Your granddaughter, Zulekha.

To my grandma, Hazel. Thank you for always showing me you love me in so many ways. You're always making sure I have good food to eat when I visit or just calling to check up on me and so much more. I hope to look as good as you when I am 92 years old.

I would like to thank God for my Spiritual Leaders who have given me guidance over my life. They offered up many prayers on my behalf and helped me grow spiritually in guides of Word and Love. In my early years in Virginia, Bishop Marjorie Ruffin of Living Water Tabernacle Baptist Church and my current Bishop, Bobby R. Weston, Sr., and Lady Aurelia Weston of Salisbury, MD.

Chapter 1
My Life Journey Cerebral Palsy

My life as Zulekha had a very dramatic start. It began on a warm spring day in 1979. My parents were both 17 years old at the time of my birth and in their senior year of high school. My mother's water broke during class and as a result, my mother and I had to be rushed to John Hopkins in Baltimore, MD. When I was born on May 16, 1979, at 10:00 am in the morning, I weighed just 2 pounds and 3 ounces. My Mom-Mom Nellie, Pop-Pop Roger, and Great Grandmom Annie came to see me at the hospital. She prayed for all the babies on the Neo-Natal Ward my mother said. My mom told me stories and showed me pictures of myself when I was in the incubator. I was so amazed and shocked to see myself that way. From that time until now, the Lord Jesus has given me a strong spirit and will to live and to succeed. My mom and dad were able to take me home from the hospital after I had gained a weight of 14 pounds and 3 ounces.

As time passed, I continued to grow like any other toddler but, I was unable to walk independently. My parents got married on March 13, 1980, after my father received his first duty station for the Navy. My mother and I left Salisbury, MD, and temporarily stayed in Elizabeth City, NC with one of her friends. It took a month before a place was available where my father was assigned for us to go.

We moved to Beaufort, South Carolina. That's where I first started getting treatment for my legs. I was only able to walk while holding onto things around me or holding onto someone's hands. My mom said when I tried to walk, I would walk on the insides of my feet. I couldn't walk flat footed like other children my age.

During my time in Beaufort, I was seen by an Optometrist because I was also born with crossed eyes. The eye doctor who performed surgery on my eyes to correct my vision was also the doctor to diagnose me with Cerebral Palsy. At the time, I was only about 15 months old.

When my eye doctor first told my mom about my diagnosis of Spastic Dysplasia Cerebral Palsy my mother asked God a question? *"God why my child?"* Then she asked the doctor a few more questions. *How did she end up with the condition? What can we do to treat this condition? What is Spastic Dysplasia Cerebral Palsy?*

According to the Seattle Children's Hospital Website, Spastic Cerebral Palsy affects muscle movements. It involves one or two parts of the brain. This type of Cerebral Palsy can occur during the early stages of a woman's pregnancy or months later. Spastic Cerebral palsy in some cases can even appear in a child two to three years old before being diagnosed. On this website, it goes on to say,

"Spastic Cerebral palsy is not a progressive condition. It does not get worse over time. It causes the body's muscles to become tight."

This condition is also associated with learning challenges. (Seattle Children's Hospital website July 29, 2013.)

When my eye doctor diagnosed me with this condition, my parents actively started seeking treatment and therapy for me. During my childhood years, I endured multiple surgeries to help improve my condition and quality of life. For example, I had two eye surgeries, my right hip was dislocated in 1990, ankle cords released, abductors released and many more surgeries to correct certain parts of my body that were affected by C.P.

I wore various types of braces to help straighten my legs and posture. I went through occupational, physical, and speech therapy in every state we lived in. I had to take speech therapy because my mom said I had to learn how to talk and breathe at the same time due to me being a mouth breather.

I started school when I was four years old. At first, I went to school in South Carolina with other kids that also had special needs. When we moved to Germantown, MD, I went to another elementary school that I enjoyed very much. This school included children that didn't have special needs. I like that because I was not separated from other kids. I really enjoyed school especially music class and making new friends since I moved around a lot.

As a child, I learned about Jesus Christ while attending our local church in MD. I accepted the Lord Jesus and was baptized at the age of ten. This was one of the best decisions I could have ever made in my life. The reason I say this is because without receiving Jesus in my life I would have been lost. My parents separated and eventually divorced. Due to these unforeseen events happening in my early life; my mother, my two brothers and I moved to Virginia. This was where I completed my high school and college education. I really feel that I had the best time of my life in high school even with Cerebral Palsy. I did not experience bullying while I was in school.

Those challenges I faced later during this stage in my life involved issues like having a date for the prom, or to the junior ring dance and passing my Algebra class. I never was asked to go out to any dances. It was always the other way around for me. When it came time for me to go to my junior ring dance, my cousin MJ was my date. I was glad he was able to go with me.

God always has a ram in the bush when it comes to times like that…I guess! I was so excited just to be able to go that I started crying because I was ready, but my date was a little late. My mom and everyone started asking me if I had ever heard of "being fashionably late?" I was not trying to hear any of that especially since this was my first important school dance, so I thought. Ring dance was great and all, but the kicker was the prom.

It was my senior year at KCS High and what time is it? Prom Fever! The guys at school were asking the girls to go to the prom with them. I really don't know why I didn't get asked by the guys I knew. I feel that it could have been they just saw me as a friend, or they already had a date. The point is I didn't get asked to go to the prom. I felt I was running out of time to

be asked so I took matters into my own hands. I asked one of the guys I was friends with at church name Darrick if he would be my prom date. To my surprise,
he replied, "*he would be honored to take me to prom.*

Darrick was in college at the time. I was over the moon excited because here I thought I was going to miss out on the most important night of all time. I had the time of my life that weekend with Darrick. He made me feel special by giving me flowers and he paid for our dinner like a true gentleman. The night after prom was my nineteenth birthday. Boy time flies by when you're having fun.

It is now my high school graduation day, June 19, 1999. I am so excited that I have finally made it to this day in spite of all of my challenges. Throughout my education, I had to be placed in special education classes. For example, English, Math, and Government. I think the smaller class setting was a good setting for me to learn because it took me longer to process information than others. I did not let the fact that I learned in a different way prevent me from getting good grades. I graduated with an honors diploma on that day with my crutches attached to my arms while holding my head high! The Lord Jesus allowed me to jump over that goal.

I can do all things through Christ which strengthens me.
(Philippians 4:13 King James version bible for women.)

I know you may have thought I was the only child but no, I have two younger brothers, Knowledge and Rod. My brothers both treated me like I didn't have Cerebral Palsy. I believe that they both enjoyed playing with whatever contraption I had to use to get around with at the time. For example, they both loved playing with my wheelchairs popping wheelies, and walking around with my crutches. Something they both liked playing practical jokes on me. One of the funny things they would do to me was when I would ask them to get me something to drink. They would instead put some kind of mystery ingredient into my drink like salt. They thought it was funny but, I didn't. Quite a few times my brothers would make me laugh so hard that I would wet myself. Guess who would get in trouble?

My brothers and me knew that if I would laugh too hard I would end up wetting my pants. We got along for the most part but, the only challenge I had was that I was not able to run after them if they took something of mine. I would fuss at them mostly, but they didn't seem to be affected by that because they would still bother with my stuff. Oh, my brothers loved when we would go to amusement parks because my disability allowed us to ride twice on all the rides. We had a blast.

My Brother's Two Cents Worth by Knowledge

For as long as I can remember, you have been a bright spot in a dark world and being that you are only three years older than me, I think it's safe to say that you were born that way. In our childhood years, my own devilment led me to believe that you never got into trouble because you could not walk but, really though it was the fact that you rarely did anything that rose to the level that punishment was necessary. Mom made it clear though that you were not above feeling the wrath of her belt and she meant it. On a few occasions when you got out of line I found it very amusing to see you squirm but even though mom didn't put her back into it like she did when me and Rod were the target! I think that's what made it funny. After hearing and seeing me and Rod get a beating you choose wisely not to do anything that would have led you to catch a beating that we caught. We as your brothers didn't make your life easy I know, but I would like to think we toughen you up a little bit. Most of the dumb things we use to do and say to make you upset were mean. I admit they were done out of immaturity and a lack of empathy, there was definitely no tolerance for anyone else messing with you through. Growing up sometimes people would ask, "what's wrong with your sister?" My reply would almost always be, ain't nothing wrong with her. She just can't walk like we walk."

You tried your best to assert your position as the oldest and it worked sometimes. Mostly when we were younger and afraid you would tell mom on us for not listening to you. When we got older you got wiser and stop letting our foolishness bother you and began focusing on doing your own thing. You have grown to be a strong intelligent young woman, who is independent, yet eager to be of service, faithful to the tenets of Christianity, and every ready with a song of praise to sing. The journey has been tough as the road has been rough but, God is concerned and He's working it out for you so blaze your trail Z.

-Donté

Aug 23, 1999, I entered college for the first time. I was very excited but nervous about this new experience because I was the first one in my immediate family to attend college. My preparation to attend college started while I was still in 12th grade. I had an advisor from my local Department of Student Services who inform me about the resources that were available for a student who was planning to attend college after high school. As a result of early college preparation, I applied for scholarships, financial aid and I was able to find out about other resources my school offered to the students with disabilities.

My freshmen year in college went by with ease except for the fact I was struggling in my Geometry class and the fact that I did not know anyone. This was a new season in my life and new territory for me. I began to pray and asked my Lord Jesus to send me some Christian friends. Guess what he did? The Lord Jesus connected me with awesome sisters in Christ. He connected me with Lakisha. We both took the same English 111 class and we sat beside each other in class. From that day forward, Lakisha and I became the best of friends. We would hang out with each other in school and even after school. We supported each other during the good times and the bad times. For example, during my second year of college, my family went through a traumatic experience.

The S.W.A.T. Team rushed into our house late one night. It was pandemonium! They had Glocks, 9mm, .40 pistols, and submachine guns drawn when they ripped through our front door. Confusion was all I could breathe not to mention I was very scared because an officer had his gun aimed right at me. As I was crawling towards the closet door, the officer yelled out to me 'don't move or I will shoot!' My mother screamed out in fear, 'please don't shoot! She's just scared and can't walk. She has Cerebral Palsy!'

They also had my youngest brother, Sharod, outside of our house on the ground because they thought he was the one they were looking for but, he wasn't. They were in fact looking for my brother Knowledge who was not at home during this chaos.

Thankfully, the officer didn't shoot me, however, I still can see the image in my mind like it just happened yesterday. The SWAT Team was looking for my other brother Knowledge. We came to learn that he had allegedly committed a horrendous crime. When Lakisha found out what we had gone through, she was right there for me lending me her ear and shoulder to cry on.

It has been 20 years later since we met, and Lakisha and I have a great time when we get together. Another great friend that Jesus blessed me with is my friend Stacy. I met Stacy after class one day while waiting for the bus to go home. We did not have any classes together, but we would eat lunch together. Stacy is a very creative person. Her passion was art and still is. One day while we were at school, she showed me some of the artwork she had been working on and it was amazing! I asked her if she could paint me a picture. She said she needs a picture of me. So, I gave her my senior photo. After some time had passed, Stacy presented me with a painted portrait of myself and I thought the portrait was awesome!

In the fall semester of 2005, the Lord Jesus allowed me to become friends with Rena during our Psychology 101 class. Rena sat beside me in class because I asked her if she could take my notes for me. She said "yes." While in Dr. Haugh's class Rena and I had a blast because Dr. Haugh made it fun and interesting. Rena always would make me laugh during class because she would pull out this big snack bag. She would have enough snacks for the entire class. One day during class Rena asked Dr. Haugh if she would like a snack and she said, "no."

Rena and I spent a lot of time laughing together inside and outside of class as well. One day after leaving psychology class, I was speeding down the hall in my motorized chair when suddenly I turned the corner to go to Dr. Haugh's office, and boom! My foot gets jammed up against the door as I turned to enter Dr. Haugh's office. I was so afraid that I had a broken leg. They called to take me to the emergency room. I wanted to go but I was concerned about how my motorized chair was going to get to the hospital with me.

Dr. Haugh assured me that my chair would get there. Thank goodness all I had was a sprained ankle. When I came back to school, Dr. Haugh and I had a story to share with the class. Everyone was wondering how I had sprained my ankle while in my wheelchair. All I could say was an accident. Overall, I am truly blessed to have great friends who became like sisters to me. While I was attending college, the most exciting event happened to me.

Jesus had blessed me with my first apartment! I had finally achieved this goal I had longed for on September 1, 2002. I was in my sophomore year of college, and I was 23 years old. My friends and family celebrated with me by giving me a housewarming party. It took me a while to get used to staying in my apartment by myself, but it soon became a way of life. Even though I was on my own now, my family and friends would still come to help me with errands I had to run when I could not take the ADA transit bus.

In college, as a freshman, my major was in Business Administration. I soon learned this wasn't the right major for me to pick because this degree required advanced math. After a long discussion with my math professor, Mrs. Hawk decided to change my degree to Human Services because it didn't require as much math. I also was advised to drop professor Hawk's Geometry class and go back to algebra.

This is when my life went from smooth sailing on an ocean to a death-defining roller coaster ride. By the time I was in my second or third year of college I was having difficulty passing the algebra classes. By now I had taken the same algebra class four times along with the help of tutors. I just was having trouble grasping the algebraic processes. During this time in my life, I was carrying a heavy burden around. I began to feel discouraged and helpless. I have always had a strong faith and belief in Jesus Christ, however, during this time in my life I felt like no one cared about what I was going through not even Jesus.

One morning as I am getting dressed for school I started crying as the radio was playing the gospel song, *I Almost Let Go*. That song made me cry because I was feeling like I could not go on with my life. That's what the Devil was placing in my head but, I knew that it was a lie. He would say, "*you know if you just kill yourself you won't have to worry about going to that math class.*" Even though I felt low that morning, I manage to go to classes, but I was not able to find my friends at school to talk to. When it was time for my mom to pick me up from school I called to talk to my friend Lakisha's Aunt Carol. I asked Aunt Carol if it was normal for me to have suicidal thoughts.

She replied, "*Yes, it was normal to have those thoughts but, she continued to tell me it's not the thoughts that are harmful. It's what you do with those thoughts.*" She continued, "*most people don't talk about them and those are the people that usually harm themselves.*"

I told her I was having trouble with passing my math classes. Suddenly Aunt Carol began to pray for me. I felt relieved that she heard my concerns and didn't pass judgment on me. Overall, I had a lot of prayer warriors who prayed for me doing this time. I finally passed the algebra class but, I had to end up switching my major because I would have had to struggle through statistics to get this degree.

I ended up graduating from college with an Associate of Science degree in General Studies. Graduating from college was even more exciting to me than graduating high school because, after having to fight with my struggles with algebra and the suicidal thoughts it brought on, I was able to look back and say, *I won and I did not give up!*

I kept pushing forward. In May of 2006, I walked with my crutches across the Hampton Coliseum Stage for the second time with my head held high to receive my Associate of Science degree in General Studies. On that day I became a local celebrity. The local newspaper wrote a news article about my college journey. My story was on the front page that weekend. It's funny how the Lord can turn a bad situation into something good!

If it wasn't for my faith in the Lord Jesus and many prayers from my church family and my immediate family, I would not have made it through that season in my life.

Now that my college career had come to a close, I was for sure that I would be able to get a good job especially since I had a college degree. Boy was I wrong! Sadly, the only job I was able to get after college was being a volunteer at one of the local hospitals in my area at the time. I was content for a while but, I wanted more for myself because I felt that I worked so hard in school for so many years.

After a year of volunteering, I decided it was time for me to look for a job that paid me money. I eventually found a job as an administrative assistant for a local company in the area. I was so proud of myself because, I finally thought I had found a great career but, this success was short-lived. I was laid off from this job after eight months. What a blow that was to my self-esteem. I felt so defeated because it seemed like the harder I tried to have a better financial situation the tougher it got for me to find a job.

Overall, since college I have had various part-time jobs but, I have been unsuccessful at finding a full-time career. One of the goals I am striving to achieve is being a motivational speaker for people who have special needs. I know that it is going to come to pass. I just have to be patient while keeping my faith walk on high.

Chapter 2
My Miracle Walk

In the Summer of 2000, I had been really praying to the Lord Jesus about some concerns I had on my heart. What is my calling and what was my purpose for being here on earth? I also asked the Lord Jesus to heal my body and my mind. Around the time my family had just gone through a traumatic event with my brother Knowledge being sent to prison.

I had a lot of questions about my life that I wanted answers to. I know the only one who had those answers was the Lord Jesus. In July of 2000, I was blessed with the opportunity to travel with my Aunt Tracey and Sister Felicia to The Woman Thou Art Loose Conference. I didn't attend many of those morning sessions because we went sightseeing, spent time in prayer, and took the time to get some much-needed rest. On the first and second night of the conference, we had to sit in the handicapped section of the Georgia Dome because I used my wheelchair on those nights of the conference. We had an overview of the entire arena except our seats were really high up. No, it was not in the nosebleed section but, it was close enough. Each night it was jammed packed with folks.

It is now the third and final day of the conference and our spirits were still fired up from all the word we had been given over the past two days. We were exhausted in our physical bodies. We did not go to the daytime session. Aunt Tracey, Sister Felecia, and I decided to take some time to pray before we left to get dinner that evening. We spent about 25-30 minutes in prayer together in our hotel room. As we were praying, we fell asleep like the disciples did when Jesus was praying in the Garden of Gethsemane.

Eventually, we woke up and got ready to go to dinner. While at dinner we talked about how awesome the messages were and how we wished we could be able to get a little closer to the bottom of the auditorium. Then Aunt Tracey and Sister Felicia came up with a bright idea. They asked me if I could walk with my crutches to the conference this time instead of using my wheelchair so we would be able to get a closer seat this way. I was very reluctant because I knew that this was not a short walk and in fact was going to be a long walk. They tried to reassure me that if I got too tired they would simply carry me. After careful and thoughtful consideration, I said I would do it. They were so happy because we would now get better seats than we had during the entire conference.

Once dinner was over, we went back to our hotel room to make sure we had everything we needed for the night. I transferred from my wheelchair to my crutches. We started our long hike to the Georgia Dome. After we left our hotel room, we took the hotel shuttle to the subway station so we could catch the train to downtown Atlanta. Once we got off of the train, we started walking on our journey which was not hard at first. I had a rhythm going. As time went on this walk to hear a message from the Lord Jesus became hard to travel. I would stop to catch my breath and rest. Then Aunt Tracey and Sister Felecia would encourage me by saying you can do it and we're almost there. Also, as we were walking the Lord Jesus sent three women to encourage and pray for me. The first two women stopped me right when I felt like I could not go on any longer.

They stopped me in my tracks to ask me if they could pray with me. I said yes to each of them. The prayer the two ladies said for me was short and sweet. They prayed for me to continue to believe and have faith that God is going to heal me. By now we were almost there, and my legs were about to give out. Aunt Tracey and Sister Felecia carried me for a little while until they could no longer carry me. I managed to finish walking to the Georgia Dome on my crutches. I was so glad to reach the doorway because I knew that I would finally be able to sit down.

The auditorium was starting to fill up with people. We were able to get seats on the lower level of the Georgia Dome instead of the upper level. It felt awesome to be there that night with so many women on one accord. The conference theme was Women Thou Art Loose! Pastor T.D. Jakes's sermon focused on the women with the issue of blood. As I was listening to the sermon that evening, I thought about the fact that I and the women with the issue of blood were similar in a lot of ways. First of all, she had spent 18 years of her life trying to find a cure for her condition.   There was no earthly cure for her condition but, she heard of a man named Jesus who healed people of their diseases. She made her way to Jesus and touched the hem of his garment and in an instant, she was made whole and healed of her condition. Like the woman with the issue of blood, I also had a condition for a long time. I was 21 years old at the time of the conference and had Cerebral Palsy all of my life now! I was hoping and praying like her for a cure for my condition. I was so encouraged by the message that I heard on that night because it gave me hope that one day I would also be healed by the Lord Jesus of Cerebral Palsy.

It was now time to leave the Georgia Dome and to travel back to our hotel room. It is now around 11:00 pm. There were hundreds of people leaving the auditorium going in many different directions. I was dreading this long walk back to get to our hotel room because we were unsure of how to get back to the train station. It was now dark, and we were not from the area, so those two factors made it challenging to find our way back. We begin to ask random people for directions to the train station but, no one could tell us how to get to the train station.

By now we were starting to get frustrated because it was late, and we were tired. Finally, someone points us in the right direction, and we were relieved. As we began our journey to the train station, it begins to drizzle. Thunder then roared in the distance. We started to walk faster than we had before because we did not want to get drenched. Thankfully we did not have to walk too much further before we entered the train station. We made it inside the train station safely, but this is when my life miraculously changed.

As we were walking towards our designated train, a woman stops me and asks could she pray for me? I nodded my head yes. Before the woman began praying for me she says,

> *"God has called you to be a prophetess over women and that many people are going be saved and healed by your testimony."*

At this point, I had come to the conclusion that the woman was an angel sent to me by God because He was the only one that knew what I had been praying about. By this time, I started crying and praising the Lord Jesus because I knew that God had in fact heard my prayers. Then the woman asked my Aunt Tracey and Sister Felecia to take my crutches away from me. The woman hugs me tightly and starts praying in my right ear repeating the same thing. *"He was wounded for my transgressions, and he was bruised for our iniquities and the chastisement of our peace was laid upon him and by his stripes, we are healed. (Isaiah. 53:5 KJV).* All of a sudden, I could feel the power of the Holy Spirit moving within me while she was still praying for me. It felt like the anointed power that she had on her was being transferred on to me.

After this, the angel who came in the form of a woman turned me around facing the crowd of people and told me to repeat her words. *"Now in the name of Jesus, I command these feet to move!"* When I released those words from my lips, my legs and feet began to run down that subway station. I ran as fast as my legs could go. I was crying and praising my Lord Jesus for what he had just done for me. As I was running all I could hear was people screaming move, move! I believe they were trying to make room for me to run. After I walked back to where my Aunt Tracey and Sister Felecia were, the woman told me to always share my testimony of what the Lord has done. She also told me that the Lord was going to finish what He started in me.

After this miraculous event in the Georgia subway station, I never saw that woman again. I truly believe that the Lord wanted to let me know that He is a healer of not just the people I read about in the biblical days but in our current days.

Once we returned home, boy did we have a story to share with our friends and loved ones. When people heard my testimony about my healing, some of them believed that it happened and some did not, because I was not walking when they saw me. After experiencing that touch from the Lord in my physical body this made my faith in Jesus stronger. For example, I shared what happened to me with some of my friends so then they wanted to help me in my walking process. A group of my friends from college would take turns walking with me after class. I would hold on to their arms or hands and walk down the hall. It was hard but I did it. Also, my healing experience showed me that there is truly nothing impossible for God. All I can say to those naysayers and those who have to see it in order to believe it, God the Father is not finished with me yet. So just wait and see!

I have always loved traveling and seeing new places and doing exciting things. In December of 2000, I was given the chance to fly to San Bernadino, California to visit family. This was exciting for me because I had never flown anywhere before let alone by myself. I had a blast because my cousins took me to Universal Citywalk, and I was able to take pictures of some of the Walk of Fame plaques. I took pictures of Bruce Lee's star as well as Michael Jackson's star. I saw lots of palm trees and I even went to the beach while was in California. It felt strange to me though because it was almost Christmas, and it was hot! No Snow in sight!

I had a great week of fun in the sun. I believe I was starting to get comfortable with the California way of living because when my mom called to see how I was doing she did not recognize my voice and said I had picked up an accent. I hope to take another trip there again soon. I am very thankful to have visited various tropical Islands over the past few years. For example, I loved St. Martin it had so many butterflies that were out while we were there. I also loved the clear blue water there.

It was so tranquil on the island. I hope to see many more places in the near future.

Lastly 2020, I was given the chance to visit San Antonio, Texas for the first time and my second time flying by myself. I was able to hang out with my cousin M and his family. I was also able to see my cousin Erica as well and had an awesome time.

Chapter 3
Keratoconus Knocks at My Door!

*Keratoconus (ker-uh-toe-KOH-nus) occurs when your cornea — the clear, dome-shaped front surface of your eye — thins and gradually bulges outward into a cone shape.
A cone-shaped cornea causes blurred vision and may cause sensitivity to light and glare. Keratoconus usually affects both eyes, though it often affects one eye more than the other. It generally begins to affect people between the ages of 10 and 25. The condition may progress slowly for 10 years or longer. (The Mayo Clinic™)

A few weeks before I found out I had this eye condition; I was very excited because I was going to be evaluated to see if I could use hand controls for driving. This was going to help when I got my license because I don't have enough flexibility in my feet to operate the foot pedals. The training facility was located in Charlottesville, VA. My friend's dad, Mr. Hogan volunteered to drive me to my training appointment due to my mom's work schedule was conflicting with my appointment.

It took about 3 ½ hours to get to Charlottesville from Hampton, VA. The training facility was very large. As I wheeled down the hall, I noticed the different work areas for testing. I was tested on my hand and eye coordination, my reaction time, my depth perception, hearing, and vision. The tests would see if I recognized street signals. The best part out of all the testing was when I had to drive the hand-controlled car they had on the property. I remember it like it was yesterday! At first, I had to get used to using the control. Once I understood how the hand control worked, I listened to the instructor while focusing on the roadway of the facility.

The instructor said I did alright; however, I would have come back because during the vision portion of the training I was having trouble reading the vision chart even with my eyeglasses on. When she told me I didn't pass, my heart was crushed because I have always wanted to drive.   She told me I will need to see my eye doctor to get my vision checked out.

A few weeks later, I went to my eye doctor to have my eyes examined. That's when I received my diagnosis of Keratoconus, a rare eye condition. Dr. Flight told me that I could get fitted for a gas permeable contact lens to help my ability to see better than with my glasses on and that this is not going to cure my newly diagnosed eye condition. He also told me he did not treat patients with Keratoconus. Then I asked him if he knew any doctor in our area who specialized in Keratoconus which he said no. Before my doctor's visit ended, I asked how much did the contacts cost? He said $250.00 per lens. Wow, I really was going to have asked the Lord Jesus to help me because my money was funny, and I didn't know what to do.

Although I was given the negative news in 2010, I continue to study very hard to get my learner's permit. One of my friends from church by the name of Mrs. Georgia took me to the DMV in Virginia to take my written test. The first time I took the test I did not pass. Since I do not believe in giving up so easily, I went back the second time. I was able to listen to the test answer by using the computer and I passed with 90%. I was so excited and proud of myself for being able to accomplish this goal.

It is now a year later after getting out of a toxic relationship I felt this push by the Holy Spirit to move. At the time I did not know where I was going but God did. On April 30, 2011, I left the Hampton Roads area and relocated to the Eastern Shore of Maryland. To my surprise, Jesus already had my footsteps planned once I stepped out on faith. No sooner than when I arrived in Maryland, my Uncle Wesley took me looking around for apartments in the area. All of a sudden, my grandma Hazel tells us to fill out an apartment application where she lived and so I obliged.   We later found out I had to wait a whole year before I could be a resident, so I lived with my mom until I was approved for an apartment where my grandma lived in Nov. 2012. During this same year, I began going to the same eye doctor's office that my grandma Hazel is a patient at, and guess what? They treat patients with Keratoconus.

Thank you, Jesus! Eventually, I was able to try out the gas permeable contact lens, even though they were difficult for me to successfully place in my eyes because. They were tiny and because of the dexterity of my fingers, this method was not going to work for me, so we discussed other options. We talked about a procedure called Corneal Cross-Linking except, it had not yet been approved by the U.S. Government.

In November of 2018, I went to a follow up visit to see how my eyes were doing. This was when my doctor discovered that my left Cornea was too thin for surgery, but my right cornea could be operated on. During this visit when my doctor left the room, I began to talk to my Lord Jesus because I needed His help. I knew I didn't have $3,000 for this surgery and it was not yet covered by insurance. I really could use a miracle during this season of my life.

Some time had passed since my visit to my Cornea specialist office when I received a call from their office They advised me that my surgery was going to be paid in full! No out-of-pocket expenses for me! I was so thankful for God the Father, Jesus, and the Holy Spirit for once again answering my prayers.

On Feb 23, 2018, the nurse and doctor assistants administered me numbing drops for my right eye along with medication to calm my nerves since I would be wide awake during the surgery. As I am laying on the bed, they placed a large metal clamp on my right eye to keep it open. They then rolled me into another room and placed me under a large microscope so my doctor could map out the area where he needed to scrape on my cornea. The doctor used a tiny spatula and scraped over the outer part of my cornea. The doctor's assistant transferred me to another room where I was later placed under ultraviolet light. The doctor then proceeded to put Riboflavin drops into my eye every five minutes. Being the inquisitive per that I am, I asked my doctor how much did the drops cost and replied $500.
I was like wow! Suddenly when I thought nothing could go wrong…it did! We were about halfway through the surgery. The ultraviolet light shuts down and the room goes dark. In my head, I'm screaming…oh no! We had to wait 30 mins for the ultraviolet light to charge back up and we were back to the operation.

The surgery was about 6 hours, give or take a few minutes, but it was successful. The recovery process was very long with many doctor's visits and eye drops. Currently, both my eyes fluctuate now between 20/70 and 20/80 so due to the fluctuation of my eyes, the doctors have determined I cannot legally drive.

Even though I've had Cornea Cross-Linking in my right eye, I have been diagnosed with low vision in both of my eyes. On September 8, 2021, I was gifted a Ruby XL by an anonymous donor who happened to be 102 years old. The Ruby XL is a portable high-tech reading device. This helps people with low vision to see what they are reading easier. This has definitely been a '*walk by faith and not by sight journey.*' -II Cor. 5:7 (NKJV).

I am still praying for the Lord Jesus to completely restore my sight.

Chapter 4
Yes, Jesus Healed Me From...

It was the beginning of 2011 when I found myself going through some tough situations. I had been diagnosed with Keratoconus in the previous year after failing my hand-controlled driving assessment. I was in a toxic relationship with a man who was not good for me, so we ended the relationship in April of 2011.

I finally went to see a dermatologist because my skin was dry and itchy and peeling off. I saw the dermatologist while living in Hampton Roads. He looked at my skin which he later diagnosed as eczema, an extreme case of it. I asked the doctor what is eczema? He said it's an inflammation of the skin characterized by redness, itchy, and oozing vesicular lesions which become scaly, crusted, and hardened. The areas that eczema affected were the tops of my hands, my neck, my eyelids, my inner arms, elbow my face, and some areas on my chest. The doctor prescribed me different topical creams and pills such as clobetasol, prednisone, and Allegra. I left this appointment feeling defeated because the doctor told me there was no cure!

As several weeks passed by, I noticed that the medicine the doctor gave me was not working. I still had the same symptoms, and it was getting worse. My skin was bleeding in some areas where the skin came off from severe itching. I could not sleep due to the internal itching sensation and external itching that was happening simultaneously with my skin. At this point, I wanted some relief and answers as well as a second opinion on what was going on with my skin. I decide to wait until I relocated to Maryland later in the month to get my second opinion.

Finally, I am settled in at my new location living with my mom until I get approved for my apartment. I asked my mom and other family members if they knew of any good dermatologists. They told me about an office in Cambridge, Maryland. I eventually was able to get an appointment with that doctor. On the day of my visit, I told the doctor what had been going on with my skin over the last several months and I also asked for a biopsy of my skin. I really liked this doctor because he listened to me and asked questions.

Dr. Brown removed a small piece of my skin for the biopsy and then prescribe some medications. He, too, also thought it was eczema but wanted to make sure. I went back to get my results and it confirmed I in fact have eczema. He said I had an extreme case just like the other doctor said back in Virginia. I let him know that the medications I was previously prescribed were not working. I tried peroxide wipes to clean my bleeding skin, prednisone, and many other remedies. Guess what happened? I still left his office with a prescription. I'm not going to bore you with the endless cycle of doctors' visits and medications I endured.

Fast forward to 2015, I was at the point of desperation one Wednesday night after bible study. I asked my pastor if he would pray for me, and he says yes. My pastor retrieved the anointing oil that came from Jerusalem, and he anoints my hands as he begins to pray for me. Afterward, my pastor tells me to anoint myself every night and watch God work. I followed my pastor's instruction with prayer and anointing myself and believe that Jesus would heal me. It was gradual but I started to notice that my skin was lightening up on all affected areas, and the itching came to an abrupt halt. I was completely healed from eczema by 2016!

Chapter 5
The Great Fall

On March 28, 2018, I was at home getting myself prepared to go to bible study when I felt led by the Holy Spirit to pray for the sick. Then out of nowhere, my phone began ringing. It was my mom calling to tell me that she was outside. I gathered my things then put my arms through the cuffs of my crutches and began walking to my back door. Suddenly, as I grabbed the doorknob to close it, I lost my balance crashing onto the concrete pavement landing in an awkward position.

I was so glad my mom was there to help me up off the ground because the pain was excruciating, especially in my left shoulder area. The pain was so intense, we decide to skip bible study and go directly to the emergency room and have my shoulder examined. While at the ER, I had an x-ray done of my left shoulder but it didn't show anything of significance. I pain was insurmountable. I ended up being prescribed medications to ease the pain then told to go see an orthopedic doctor if I still was having pain.

As days went by, my shoulder continued throbbing but this time with severe sharp pain. I was not able to raise my arm up like I normally could before I fell. I decided to see an orthopedic doctor. While at the doctor's appointment, Dr. B. evaluated my range of motion and asked me about my health history. He then gave me a script to have an MRI done of my shoulder.

It's been a few days since I have had my MRI done and was soon scheduled to go back to Dr. B's office and get my results. I was began praying to myself diligently.
"Lord Jesus please don't let it be nothing too serious."

Boy, was I wrong! I learned from the doctor that I have a 2/1/2-inch tear on my left shoulder.

When I first hear the news about the tear in my shoulder, I was not happy because I knew I did not want to deal with that pain for the rest of life. Dr B. goes on to explain that I had two options to resolve this tear. First option was to have physical therapy and try cortisone shots to help with pain and leave the tear alone. The second option was to have it repaired with shoulder and physical therapy. He was very compassionate of any decision I make would be my decision and mines alone. He told me and mom to give his office a call after I had made my final decision.

After numerous prayers and discussions, I decided to go through with the latter option. On October 11, 2018, I had surgery to have my left rotator cuff repaired. Yes, I was a little nervous but, my Aunt Tracey and mom prayed for me the entire time with everything ending up fine. This was my twelfth surgery I had in my life. The only difference with this surgery process from others was the fact that I was given a nerve block before surgery to help with the pain.

The anesthesiologist came in my room with his assistant to help when he gave me the nerve blocker. It felt funny because they were pointing and prodding me to find my nerve, and once they found it, I was then wheeled down to the operating room. Once there, I asked the assistant if he could wait until I was asleep to place the mask over my face. He obliged. The next thing I know I was out for the count! My mom informed me the doctor said the surgery went well.

Chapter 6

The Seaside Rehabilitation

I was moved to the Seaside Regional Rehabilitation hospital four days later after my shoulder surgery. I was ready to get the healing process over and done with. The medical transportation driver asked the receptionist which room was I supposed to be staying in and she responded I was going to room 194 D, which was down the hall on the right. Upon entering the room, I got settled into my bed, I was greeted by nurses and doctors. Immediately, they began taking my vital signs and asked me various health questions since I was a new patient.

Once the doctors and nurse had finished with my initial exam I was finally able to talk to my mom who had just come to visit me. During all the commotion in my room, I noticed that I had a roommate. As my mom and I was deep in conversation about our day, all of a sudden, I heard my roommate Susan tell the nurse I talked too much. I was on my side of the room might I add. I quickly peered over at my mom standing there beside me. I then began saying a small prayer. From this point on, I had a feeling this place was going to be a test of my faith and time. So, the fun had just begun!

I had a very difficult time adjusting to my new surroundings. I did not enjoy having to get up earlier while I was there because I didn't get enough sleep as is thanks to various situations that occurred at night. Also, I was not used to having someone help me with going to the bathroom, dressing, and many other basic needs.

While at the rehabilitation facility, my daily routine was getting help with bathing, being dressed by nurses and or by my occupational therapist, Bethany. After I was dressed, I would have breakfast and then commence to daily sessions with different occupational and physical therapists.

I then got a break for lunch and if I was done with all of my sessions, I would return to my room.

As the days went on, I was getting stronger every day that I was there. I showed the doctors and nurses that I could push myself with my right arm down the hall after about the second week of being there. Jesus was performing many miracles during my healing process. He allowed me to get strong enough to be able to put on my arm sling by myself and eventually able to shower and dress with minimal help. I also had learned how to transfer from my wheelchair to my bed, to the toilet, and even a car while my arm was in a sling. It was a gradual process that took a lot of determination and prayers to get me through.

I was finally discharged, after 27 days of physical and occupational therapy. I was anxious to get home to my peaceful apartment. I would be forever grateful for the therapists whom I had the opportunity to meet throughout this journey, but it was time to go home. My therapy journey did not end here as I had to continue with outpatient therapy.

Chapter 7
Stony Brook Physical Therapy

My healing process for my shoulder continued on when I became a patient at Stony Brook PT. On December 4, 2018, I was so excited and determined to get started with physical therapy because I wanted to be able to walk with my crutches again. I knew that I was going to have to lean and depend on my Lord and Savior Jesus for strength, guidance, and wisdom during the times when I felt weak.

During my first visit as a new patient, the head therapist Janice had to assess my physical abilities, strengths, and weaknesses of my body. She also asked me what I was able to do before my fall. I told Janice that I used the hopping or otherwise known as the swing through method when I used my crutches. At first she did not understand my description so I had to pull up my YouTube channel '*Zulekha Jones*' to show her what I was talking about.

When she saw my video called, "Zee on the Move," she said, "oh now I see." I told her that I had been walking this way from age 10 to 39. As we continued our conversation, I informed Janice that I wanted to learn how to walk using the crutch foot method instead of the swing through method so my legs could gain strength along with my arms. She told me she was going to focus on strengthening my left arm along with my legs. Eventually I would walk with my crutches again, however, she let me know it was going to be a gradual process. Before leaving my initial PT visit, I was given some exercises and TheraBands to work out with at home. Boy was this going to be an uphill battle.

As I continued my physical therapy 2-3 times a week, my abilities and strength progressed. For example, at first I still had to continue using my arm sling when I was moving but, after six weeks, Doctor B. said I didn't need to wear the arm sling anymore. This was music to my ears because it meant I didn't have to wear it to bed or during the day. I thank my Lord Jesus for getting me to this point because without Him, I would not have made it. The next big transformation I went through during my PT session occurred on January 10, 2019.

My therapist asked if I could stand up and take a few steps. As she stood behind me, she held onto my transfer belt situated around my waist to make sure I didn't fall. The other therapist had pushed my wheelchair nearby. I was very excited yet scared because it had been seven months since I had last walked. First, I stood up slowly to get my bearings and then I did the crutch foot method of walking. It felt weird to me at first because I was not used to it, but the more I was persevered, the more it became easier. This was a wonderful day in my healing process because the Lord Jesus gave me the strength to walk 202 feet!

Every time I went to physical therapy, I would learn a new exercises to help strengthen my body. As my legs became stronger, I learned how to do squats for the first time in my life. I just would hold onto a bar in front of me then bend down and rise back up it was slow going at first but, I eventually comprehended it. The other area I became better with was my walking distance. I was getting further every time.

On January 15, 2019, I was able to walk 264 feet with my new style of walking. Wow it was amazing to watch the Lord Jesus give me the strength and endurance to keep passing each goal.

The best part about my therapy sessions at Stony Brooke occurred when they allowed me to use the [1] Alter-G or Anti-Gravity Treadmill™. What is the Alter-G or Anti-Gravity machine? The pressurized mechanics of the treadmill act to "unweight" the patient up to 80% of their body weight while the machine is in use. By doing so, the patient is able to use the treadmill by seemingly "floating" above it–allowing them to complete their exercise without the harsh foot-to-treadmill impact you get with normal gravity. The Differential Air Pressure (DAP) technology has been patented by NASA, allowing for a precise calibration of air

---

[1] Tennessee Sports Medicine Group. Article online 11/29/2021 https://tennsportsmed.com/physical-therapy-treatments/alter-g-anti-gravity-treadmill/

pressure which aids in helping those who have injuries to their lower extremities that can put their full body weight on it.

The first time I used the Alter-G Treadmill, I had to put on these special shorts and then my therapists wheeled my chair close to the treadmill. Then I had to stand up and step on to the treadmill and they zipped up the lower half of my body in the machine. The cool part of this process was when the machine measured your body weight then it takes half or all of the person's body weight off. My first time on this machine it felt as if I was walking on the air or clouds like the astronauts aboard a NASA spacecraft bound for orbit and beyond. I didn't feel any pain nor spasticity from the Cerebral Palsy while walking on Alter-G. because gravity removed majority of my body weight. The first time using the Alter G, I was only able to stay on it for a few minutes because my legs were tired.

By the time March rolled around, I had reached all of my goals for my shoulder recovery. I was able to walk on the Alter-G for 10 minutes with one pause break in between. I really wish I could afford to have one at home but, they are very expensive. My physical therapy sessions ended on March 26, 2019, but I continued my new walking exercises I had learned at home.

Chapter 8
My Traveling Shows

One fun fact about me is that I love to travel in spite of my Cerebral Palsy and other challenges. I didn't let these things get in my way when I ventured to new places to see different sites not to mention meeting new people. I've learned that I must plan ahead and make sure that where I'm going is handicap accessible. For instance, when I went on a cruise, I had to take my folding wheelchair with me and my loft strain crutches so I could move about in our cabin and other areas on the ship. Did I say I went on a cruise? Yes, I have been on a total of three carnival cruises.to be exact.

The first cruise that I ever went on was when I was in the 11th grade. Our choir in high school was the first school to ever go out of United States on The Disney Cruise™. My choir teacher, Ms. Forrest told me that the reason we went on this cruise was because we were in a competition and guess what? We won a gold medal and we had a remarkable time on this trip.

The second cruise I went on was also to the Bahamas but this time it was with family. During this trip I was able to purchase my first gemstone which happens to be a purple amethyst ring. I was able to go on the beach and get into the water. It was amazing! It was so relaxing. I felt like the lady in the Calgon commercial…take me away!

My last and final cruise I went on was the Southern Caribbean cruise which we went on in 2015. This was also a family cruise. A very special one. The reason I say this is because my grandfather Roger was there on this cruise. On this cruise, we traveled to St. Lucia, Saint Martin, Saint Kitts, and Saint Thomas. We were on a Christmas 7 Day cruise. The best part about this cruise was when we were able to go to Saint Martin and I was pushed in my wheelchair close to the water. I then used my crutches to walk and sit in the clear blue water which I loved so much. I also loved the beautiful butterflies that flew around us as we were on the island.

This was a sight to behold. While we were at the beach, I was acting like I was a swimsuit model just enjoying the beach and the clear blue water. I stayed in the water for about two hours. I'm not a water baby at all. I am normally a scaredy cat but while on the island, I loved being in the water because not only could I see my feet at the bottom, I also knew I would not drown. It was just a great feeling to know that I was in paradise on this beautiful island enjoying the breeze that was blowing in between my braids. It was a great moment.

One fond memory that I will always remember was that my Grandpop Roger even, at 80 years old, he had traveled the world, too. Each island we visited, he got off the ship just so that he could say he had been on each island. Sadly, this would be the last cruise we would ever travel together. On July 30, 2021, my beloved Grandpop passed away.

Some other trips I went on while in high school was my senior class trip for choir. We went to New York City. We were able to go to a couple of Broadway shows and go see all the tourist parts of New York. We were able to go to the top of the Empire State Building. We went to see the Twin Towers as well as the bottom half of the Statue of Liberty and it was astounding! I even went inside The Rockefeller Center and ate at Planet Hollywood.

As you can see I had lots of fun filled field trips. When I was in 7th grade, our history class was able to visit each state along the East Coast from Virginia to Maine. We got to see all the battle grounds of the Civil War and the Battle of Gettysburg. We saw so many amazing East Coast states. The trips were truly amazing trip. I will never forget them.

It has been challenging to travel for me in 2020 due to the COVID pandemic. Everything ceased for the most part. In November of 2020 I was able to go to San Antonio, Texas to visit my cousin M and his family. This was my second time traveling on a plane by myself since 2000. It was a little scary at first due I hadn't been traveling by myself since my California trip but, I needed a break.

On this trip, I learned that I was able to take along my manual wheelchair and my crutches. I was escorted to my gate by an airport escort along with my mom. She made sure I got on the plane safely and then she waved her goodbyes. The airplane and airline staff were all very courteous meeting all my needs that I had during my flight. I didn't have to be concerned with connecting flights which was a blessing because that would have been a different story. Overall, the flight was great. In case you are wondering, my reservations were made by my family on my behalf. I really enjoyed my time in San Antonio, Texas. I spent time enjoying the warm heat of the sun that I didn't have in my home state of Maryland. I did a little shopping with my cousin Erica. We went to the famous hamburger restaurant. I also enjoyed Boba tea which I never had before.

In the near future I hope to travel to many more places and faraway lands. My next destinations are to visit Hawaii and Tahiti. I know that sounds strange but, I would like to go anywhere that's warm and have tropical breeze and blue Kool-Aid water.

Well, this is the end of my excursions for now. I hope after you read this chapter about places that I have traveled, you will realize that there are so many places to go out into the world and see. Hopefully you wouldn't want to be stuck in the same town or in one place.

You must tell yourself to go out and see what the world has to offer and discover life.

Stay Blessed and Prosperous!

Author, Zulekha I. Jones

About the Author

"I beseech you therefore, brethren, by the mercies of God, that ye present your bodies a living sacrifice, holy, acceptable unto God, which is your reasonable service." -Romans 12:1 (King James Version)

The purpose of my autobiography is to give the reader a brief glance inside of my life which chronicles the many physical, emotional, and spiritual challenges I've had to overcome during my 42 years of life with cerebral palsy. I had to depend on my strong faith and devotion to Jesus Christ to see me through many torrential storms.

I have created my own YouTube channel, Zulekha Jones. I am currently striving to reach my goal to become a motivational speaker. I hope to encourage many people, that have various types of challenges in their lives.

Contact Information for Zulekha I. Jones

Email: **Zeepurple37@gmail.com**

f **Zulekha Jones**

◎ **@joneszulekha**

You Tube **Zulekha Jones**

Zulekha's BornDay!

Me in the incubator
May 16, 1979

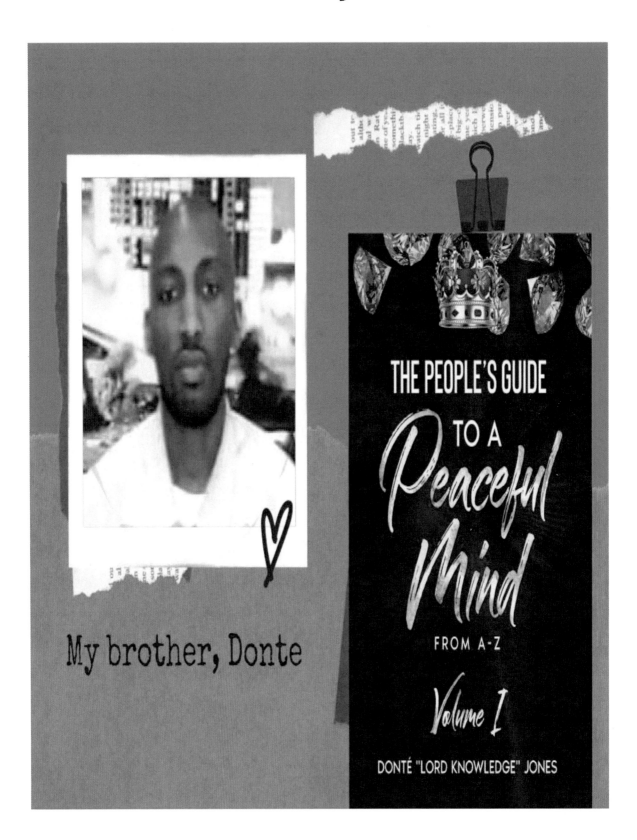

My brother, Donte

THE PEOPLE'S GUIDE TO A *Peaceful Mind* FROM A-Z

Volume I

DONTÉ "LORD KNOWLEDGE" JONES

Church Days ♡

Me and My Cousin Anyae

Me

Me

Me and Lakisha

Me and Mom

My Prom

It's Me!

It's Me!

My Graduation from Kecoughtan High School

Favorite things about me.

- My Love for Jesus Christ

- My smile

- I love learning new things

Me on my 11th Grade Disney Cruise

Me in the Southern Caribbean

Dear Cousin M,

Thank you for being there for me during my Ring Dance.

Your Cousin,
Zulekha

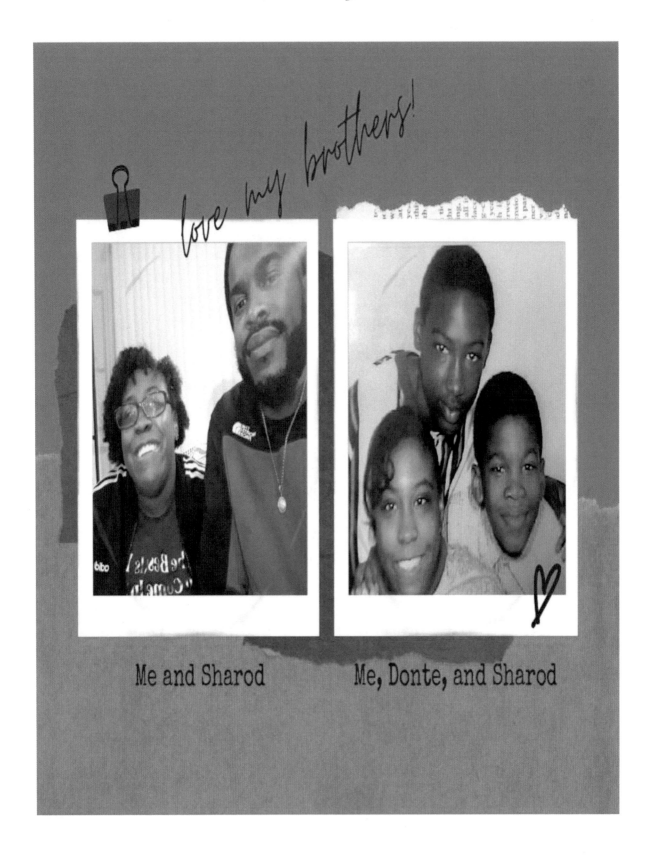

Me and Sharod   Me, Donte, and Sharod

L-R

Aunt Monica, Mom (Mabeline), Pop Pop Roger Polk, Sr., Aunt Tracey

Me and my bestie, Lakisha

Friends that pray together, stays together

Me and my bestie, Rena

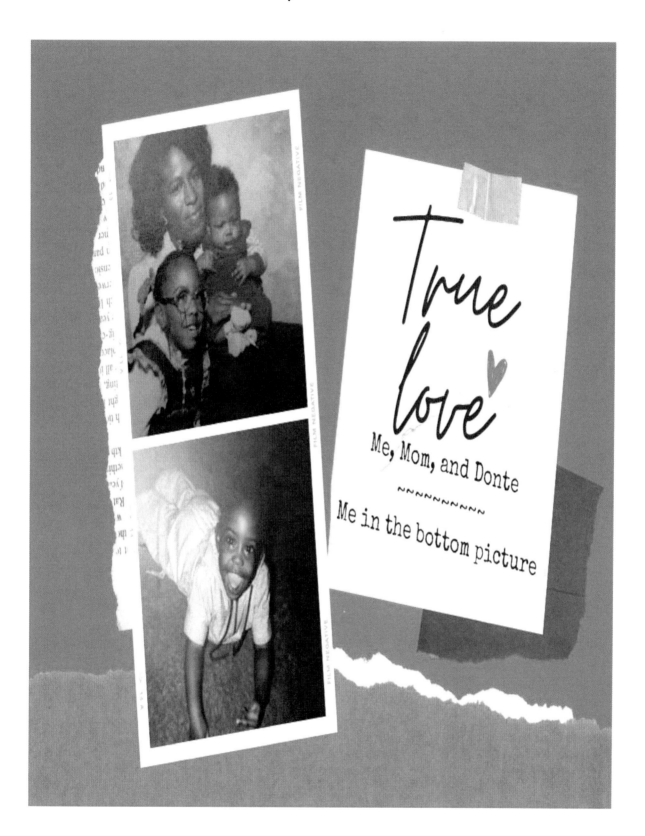

True
love

Me, Mom, and Donte
~~~~~~~~~~

Me in the bottom picture

Me and Grandma

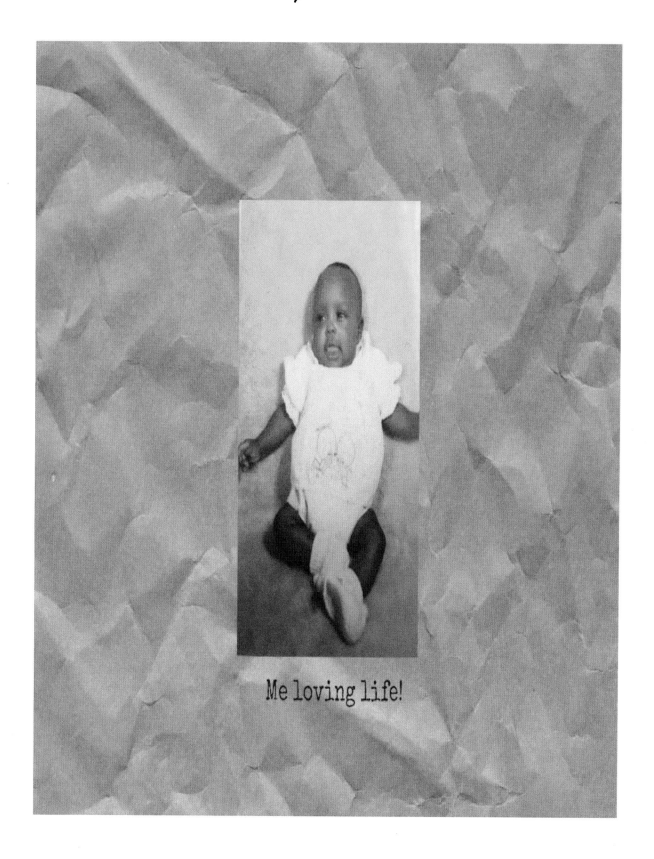

Me loving life!

My first months of life

Me and Mom   Mom, Dad, and Me

Aunt Tracey and Me

*The picture above is depicting a woman with hand crutches defying the odds proving one main fact:

" *I can do all things through Christ which strengtheneth me.*"
-**Philippians 4:13 (KJV)**

www.VanderbiltMediaHouse.net

Made in the USA
Middletown, DE
23 April 2022